Things They Carry

Cristie Arguin

BookLeaf
Publishing

India | USA | UK

Presentation by *BookLeaf Publishing*

Web: www.bookleafpub.com

E-mail: info@bookleafpub.com

ISBN: 9789360944780

First edition 2024

Emma, you are my joy and my original inspiration, so I dedicate this book to you. I hope your teaching journey fills your heart as well.

ACKNOWLEDGEMENT

Thank you, Mike, for supporting my writing time. Thank you to my students for inspiring me everyday.

PREFACE

Students come into school everyday filled with so many emotions, so many needs, and, in spite of that, we need to find a way to teach and to reach them all.

Things They Carry

Each year they come,
Carrying backpacks filled with
Trauma
Hunger
Sadness
Rejection
Fear and
Longing.
Hats and hoodies
covering their heads scream,
"Leave me alone!"
But I won't.

Math Problem

Fractions and decimals laughed
As they danced across the page.
Looking left to right, then up and down
No connection, no sense,
Only memories of failure.
His brain froze
He filled with anxiety
He tried to remember anything
He touched his pencil to the page
Nothing
He gave up
His hooded head now sits upon his Math.

English Problem

Mr. Jackson asked me
About me.
How dare he!
"What do you want to do after graduation?"
Seriously, rude!
It's none of his business!
He asks us to share our words.
How could he?
My words are my own.
My thoughts are my thoughts.
My dreams are…
Non-existent.
I don't know how to live in this world.

Cut

Bracelets and long sleeves
Cover my work
Feelings gather just under my skin
Shallow cuts bleed them out of me
And then I can breathe.

Rage

"If she asks me again,
I'm gonna punch her in the fucking face!"
Sit and breathe
Breathe in
Breathe out
Wait
Calm will return.

Inappropriate

"*He* touched me."
I didn't like it. It reminded me
Of that other time
That's been eating my soul
Filling my dreams
Darkening my spirit.
If I say it
What will happen?
I'll try this instead,
"*He* touched me."

Trust

I trusted her.
I told her the truth
And she lied
To my family
To my teachers
To my friends.
I've been
Cast out
Removed from
Banned
Exiled
All because
I trusted her.

No one

8

No one understands.
I walk slowly
I go alone
I say nothing
I expect nothing
I do as I'm told.
I try to answer
Questions meaning
Nothing more than to
Assuage guilt.
No one understands.

Hungry

9

I didn't bring a snack today;
That's what the teacher noticed.
I didn't have breakfast,
Or dinner last night, either.
My stomach hurts. I shut my eyes;
I put my head down, too.
Lunch is very far away.
I am hopeless, I withdraw.
That's what the teacher noticed.
I can't see the words on the page.
I can't hear the words she's saying.
I walk away and look out the window.
That's what the teacher noticed.

VAPE

Venomous Vapors fill my lungs,
Aiming to Attempt Addiction.
Poisonous, Propylene glycol
Exhaled, Exhausted, E-hookahs.

School

I can't wait to go to school today.
It's bad again.
Mom smiles without him here
She reads me books and we dance.
When he comes, I stay
Quiet
Away
Still
I can't wait to go to school today.
He's back again.
Mom makes dinner without him here
She makes dessert and we eat.
When he comes, I don't
Sleep
Eat
Move
I can't wait to go to school today.

In My Room

12

I am in my room
I dance
I read
I write
I dream
I am me in my room
I try on clothes
I practice with makeup
I play with my hair
I check my smiles
I am enough in my room
No one sees me
No one talks to me
No one judges me

A Blank Page

13

I don't know where to begin.
There is only white in front of me-
No lines
No numbers
No questions
The teacher says, "Just start."
Start?
With what
With who
With how
WTF?

Favorite Teacher

14

Each morning, frustrated
I enter his room
He has time for me.
At lunch
I sit alone so
He sits with me.
In class
I don't understand so
He instructs me.
Before dismissal
I'm anxious to go home
He assures me.

Josie

Josie used to talk to me
She used to be my friend.
I told all I wanted to be
And who I liked for men.
Josie walks right by me now
She pretends that I'm not here.
If only she would tell me how
To recover a friend so dear.

John

John has deserted his friends
They said, "Quit or you can't come."
He chose to stay and be by himself.
John has stopped going to school
They said, "Come or you can't graduate."
He chose to stay home.
John isn't joining his family for dinner.
They said, "Sit or find your own food."
He chose to stay in his room.
John isn't himself anymore.
They said, "Come with us and be yourself."
He chose to join
John isn't sober anymore.

Mirror

In you I see me
Together we are we
Alone I am me
With all we are free

Target

I barely exist
I'm too ashamed to go to school
Others' words ruin my life
I don't know what is wrong
Are my clothes not right?
Am I ugly?
Why can't I be like them?
They pretend I'm not here
Or they laugh at me.

I Wish You Knew

19

I wish you knew
I wish I could escape
I wish this heavy weight would leave
I hold it in so tight
I hold my hands in fists
I hold you, but you don't know
I wish you knew this
Then I could be free.

Disorderly

Sometimes I lose control.
I can't help it
Please understand!
Why won't you stop yelling?
I want to finish that!
I need to do this now…
STOP!
I'm out!
Please let me back.
I want to finish.

RTCC

21

I hated school
I had to sit
I had to listen
Then I found my home.
Here I learn by example
I work with my hands
I am challenged
I am engaged
I am learning a trade
I love this school.

* 9 7 8 9 3 6 0 9 4 4 7 8 0 *